Copyright © 2021 by Claire Sinclair and Amir Achitoov

All rights reserved. No part of this publication may be reproduced, distributed, or transmitted in any form or by any means, including photocopying, recording, or other electronic or mechanical methods, without the prior written permission of the publisher, except in the case of brief quotations embodied in critical reviews and certain other noncommercial uses permitted by copyright law. For permission requests, write to the publisher, addressed "Attention: Permissions Coordinator," at the address below.

ISBN: 978-1-7330875-7-5

Book design by Amir Designs, LLC. Millburn, NJ
First print edition 2021
Amarna Books & Media
Maplewood, New Jersey
www.amarnabooksandmedia.com
www.squeakyandcheesy.com

There was a school in town.
It was old and quiet and small.
Inside was a very big secret
And it was hidden behind a wall.

All summer those mice played freely,
When no people were in sight,
They would run around the classroom
In the daytime and at night!

They loved the reading corner
And the sandbox was lots of fun!
But their very favorite thing to do
Was run and run and run!

They would go inside the dollhouse,
And play in the wooden block bin,
They never were seen or spotted,
Since no one ever looked in.

But then it was September,
And the room grew very loud!
The classroom filled with children—
A very noisy crowd!

The noise was really frightening,
And it hurt their little ears.
They stayed quiet behind the wall
And tried to calm their fears!

They tried not to be spotted,
They tried to not be seen,
They knew if someone caught them,
Some people could be mean!

But when all was calm and quiet,
And the children had left for the day,
The mice would come back out
And once again would play!

They'd scoot out of their corner,
And crawl upon the floor
But they would always stay away
From the windows and the door.

They had heard some scary stories
About people not liking mice,
"What's not to like?"
      the little mice thought
They felt that they were nice!

It made them sad to think that
They may not be wanted there.
They saw how happy the children were
With their teacher, Ms. Pierre.

But once a day the room grew quiet,
As the children sat on the rug,
And the mice would peek their heads
Out of the tiny hole they dug.

For several days those little mice
Would leave their hiding place,
They'd listen to the teacher's voice,
And watch her gentle face.

They'd sit under the table
Very quietly side by side.
At first, they were quite careful
Making sure that they weren't spied!

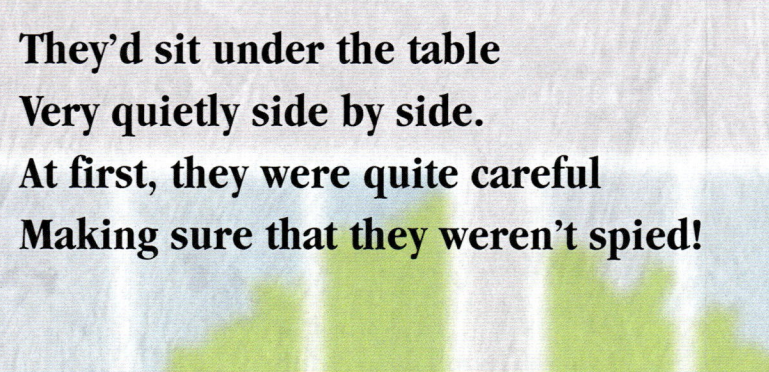

Perhaps those mice got too relaxed,
For one day they ran out.
Before they knew what was going on,
There was mayhem all about!

The moment they were spotted,
It was Tashi who screamed in fear,
"Where did they come from?" Ellie asked.
"How did they get in here?"

The mice were very frightened
And they ran back to the wall,
Terrified that they'd been seen.
Not by one but by them all!

Ms. Pierre calmed down the class,
And she told them, "Keep it down."
Some were smiling and laughing a bit
But others could only frown.

"Let's talk about what we saw,
   my friends"
Ms. Pierre said to her class.
"Those mice were
   just as scared as us.
Let's let a few moments pass."

"I don't think I want them here!"
Alfonso shouted out.
"They make me feel all nervous!"
And he gave a little pout.

"I hope they do come back!" Joon said
"Those mice were super sweet!
Maybe we could leave them
Some kind of special treat!"

"Great idea!" Elijah said.
"Let's see if they come back.
We can wait and watch and maybe
Tempt them with a snack!"

"What happens if we do not tell,
And we let them come again?
Do you think we'll get in trouble?"
Asked a little girl named Jenn.

"I'm going to leave it up to you."
Ms. Pierre said. "Let's all vote."
She had the children raise their hands
And she wrote it on a note.

She tallied up all their answers
When they told her no or yes.
As she counted all their votes,
The no's had many less.

And so it was decided
That for now they wouldn't tell.
They'd wait to see what happened
And hope it all went well!

Carlos said,
  "Let's give them names!"
Christine said, "We need two!"
The classroom filled with chatter
As the kids' excitement grew.

They talked about it quite a bit
But it was agreed on them by all.
Squeaky and Cheesy were chosen.
Great names for mice so small.

The next day during story time
The children left a plate.
They put it near the table
Wondering just how long they'd wait.

On the plate there was a raisin,
And a piece of cheese so small,
A cracker and a berry,
A bit of something from them all.

The mice were filled with wonder,
Could they creep out just a bit,
Should they crawl out to the table,
And find a place to sit?

So very, very slowly
They wandered out again,
And nervously they went and sat
Behind a kid named Ben.

"Shh, be quiet! Don't make a sound."
Whispered DJ, quietly.
"I think they want to hear some more,
And they want to sit near me!"

From that day on at story time,
Those little mice came out,
They sat beside the children
Feeling loved without a doubt!

Until just now that secret was kept
Within the classroom walls.
But what do you think might happen
If the mice wander...

Dedicated to
Dave, DJ and Drew
and
All of the students
who have passed through the doors of Room 123.
This is for you.

And to all the mice
that were totally misunderstood
when all they wanted was to live their humble lives.

And also to **Lori, Mia and Lily**
that will certainly run and scream
if they see a real one.

After more than 25 years of reading to her students, **Claire Sinclair**, mom, Kindergarten teacher and lover of children's books, decided to finally write one of her own! **The Mice Who Came to Story Time** is loosely based on the mice who would occasionally appear in her classroom.

This is the very same classroom where Claire herself attended Kindergarten as a child. The room where mice have been making appearances long before she was ever there!

Amir Achitoov was born many years ago in Israel 'with a brush in his hand'. Since he can remember he was drawing and painting.

Amir studied fine art in Holland and New York City, and held several oil painting and pastel exhibitions.

When he doesn't draw, paint or illustrate, Amir creates art for other projects. And when he doesn't do that, he is usually busy with his loving family…

Visit us at
www.squeakyandcheesy.com

"I shall do nothing of the sort," said the Mouse, getting up and walking away. "You insult me by talking such nonsense!" "I didn't mean it!" pleaded poor Alice. "But you are so easily offended!"

The mouse only growled. "Please come back and finish your story!" Alice called after it. And the others all joined in chorus. "Yes, please!" But the mouse only shook its head impatiently, and walked a little quicker. "What a pity it wouldn't stay!" sighed

Made in United States
North Haven, CT
22 November 2021